Babe
Didrikson Zaharias

Babe
Didrikson Zaharias
All-Around Athlete

by Jane Sutcliffe
illustrations by Jeni Reeves

M Millbrook Press/Minneapolis

Special thanks to my models for Babe Didrikson: Ann Adams for the young Babe and Chris Puk for the older Babe. Thanks to the following people and organizations for providing information and resources: Charlotte Holliman of the Mary and John Gray Library; Joe Scamberger of the Babe Didrikson Zaharias Foundation; Rosemary Cox of the Babe Didrikson Zaharias Museum; Rhonel and April Didrikson; Jonathan Gerland of the Tyrrell Historical Library in Beaumont, Texas; Paulette Hasier of the Dallas Public Library; Kevin B. Leonard of Northwestern University Library; and Celia Hilliard of the Chicago Woman's Athletic Club. — J. R.

The photograph on page 47 appears courtesy of Archive Photos.

This book is available in two editions:
Library binding by Millbrook Press, a division of Lerner Publishing Group, Inc.
Soft cover by First Avenue Editions, an imprint of Lerner Publishing Group, Inc.
241 First Avenue North, Minneapolis, MN 55401 USA

For reading levels and more information, look up this title at www.lernerbooks.com.

Library of Congress Cataloging-in-Publication Data

Sutcliffe, Jane.
    Babe Didrikson Zaharias: all-around athlete / by Jane Sutcliffe; illustrations by Jeni Reeves.
        p.   cm. — (Carolrhoda on my own biography)
    Summary: Tells the story of this athlete's early life, All-Star basketball career, and winning of three medals in track and field at the 1932 Olympics.
    ISBN 978-1-57505-421-6 (lib. bdg. : alk. paper)
    ISBN 978-0-7613-5828-2 (eBook)
    1. Zaharias, Babe Didrikson, 1911–1956—Juvenile literature.
2. Athletes—United States—Biography—Juvenile literature.
[1. Zaharias, Babe Didrikson, 1911–1956. 2. Athletes. 3. Women— Biography.] I. Reeves, Jeni, ill. II. Title. III. Series.
GV697.Z26S88 2000
796.352'092—dc21
[B]   99-27486

Manufactured in the United States of America
4 - 36859 - 3982 - 3/22/2017

For John and Michael, who were the beginning
— J. S.

To another great all-arounder, Tegan Reeves
— J. R.

Doucette Street
Beaumont, Texas, 1919

Babe ran as fast as she could.

Her mother needed something

from the store.

Going to the store for Momma

was eight-year-old Babe's special job.

She ran all the way.

Babe didn't stop, even when she got
to the store.

She just called out her order as she ran.

The store clerk knew Babe.

He tossed her what she wanted.

That way Babe didn't have to slow down.

She just caught the package
and kept going.

Sometimes Babe didn't just run to the store.
She jumped, too.
She liked to jump over the prickly hedges
between the houses.
Babe kept her front leg bent
so she wouldn't get scratched.

One neighbor's hedge was higher
than the others.
Babe had to go around that one.
One day, Babe asked the man
if he would mind cutting his hedge.
The man listened, then he did it.
After that, nothing got in the way
of Babe's jumping.

Babe was born in 1911.

Her real name was Mildred Ella Didrikson.

Hardly anyone called her Mildred, though.

Her mother called her Baby.

The neighborhood children said
she could hit a baseball like
"a regular Babe Ruth."

From then on, everyone called her Babe.

There were seven children
in the Didrikson family.
With such a big family,
there wasn't much money for extras.

For fun, Poppa built a gym
in their backyard.
He put up bars for jumping and for chinning.
A broomstick became a barbell.
Poppa built the barbell for Babe's brothers.
But Babe didn't care.
She knew she was just as strong as any boy.
She was just as fast, too.
She always beat the neighborhood boys
in races.
She was picked first
for every baseball game.
When the boys played football,
she played, too.

More than anything, Babe loved running,
jumping, and throwing.
She liked to turn everything into a game.
When it was Babe's turn to scrub the floor,
she strapped the scrub brushes to her feet.
Then she skated on the soapsuds.

When Momma sent her on errands,
Babe raced the streetcars from stop to stop.
And she always ran to win.
Babe didn't just want to be an athlete.
She wanted to be the greatest athlete
that ever lived.

One day, Poppa read an exciting story
in the newspaper.

It was 1928.

The Olympic Games were being held
in Amsterdam, Holland.

Poppa read to the children about the
star athletes from all over the world.

Babe listened.

Her eyes were wide.

Her heart beat wildly.

The Olympic athletes were doing
what she loved best.

And they were winning medals for it!

To Babe, it sounded like the greatest thing
in the world.

She told her family that someday
she would be in the Olympics, too.

Beaumont High School, 1928

"Babe! Babe!" the crowd chanted.

Babe's teammate passed her the ball.

Sixteen-year-old Babe shot for the basket.

She scored!

The crowd cheered.

They were used to seeing Babe score

for Beaumont High School.

She wasn't very tall,

but she was their best player.

She often scored 30 to 40

points a game.

Reporters began to write
about the schoolgirl star.
In Dallas, "Colonel" M. J. McCombs
read the articles.
He managed a women's basketball team
called the Golden Cyclones.
In February 1930, McCombs offered Babe
a spot on his team.

Babe was eager to go.

She would have to leave school
to move to Dallas.

But McCombs promised she could finish
school when basketball season was over.

Momma and Poppa agreed.

They knew how much Babe wanted
to play on a real team.

On Babe's first night in Dallas,

she played her first game for the Cyclones.

All by herself, she scored more points

than the other team did.

Babe became the star

of the Golden Cyclones that year.

She was named an All-American

basketball player.

That meant she was one of the

best players in the country.

After finishing high school,
Babe went back to Dallas.
She took a job
at Colonel McCombs's company.
During the day, she typed.
After work, she played basketball.

McCombs wanted Babe to try
other sports, too.
One day he took her
to a track-and-field meet.

Babe had never been to a meet before.
McCombs explained the events to her.
Babe liked the hurdles best of all.
They reminded her of the hedges
she had jumped back home.

McCombs helped the Golden Cyclones
form a track-and-field team.
The first meet was only a few days away.
That didn't leave much time to practice.
Most of the women chose one event.
Babe entered four events.
She won all four.

All that summer, Babe worked hard
to make her skills even better.
She kept practicing long after her team-
mates had gone home.
Sometimes she practiced by moonlight.
And she kept on winning.

Soon Babe was setting new records
in the high jump, the javelin,
and the baseball throw.
Newspapers started calling her
the "Texas Tornado."

Babe won gold medals at all her meets
that summer and the next.
She kept playing basketball, too.
She was named an All-American player
again in 1931 and 1932.

By early 1932, Babe had begun to think
about the Olympics again.
The track-and-field national championship
meet was coming up.
The winners would go on
to the Olympics that year.
Colonel McCombs sent Babe alone
to represent the Golden Cyclones.
She was the whole team.
There were 10 events at the meet.
Babe was entered in 8 of them.
But she wasn't worried.
She later said it was one of those days
when she felt "just right."
She felt as if she could fly.

For three hours, she flew from event to event.
Sometimes the judges had to wait
to let Babe catch her breath.
One of her events was the shot put.
Babe had hardly ever practiced it before.
It didn't matter.
Babe won, and she set a national record.
She broke world records
in three other events, too.

Altogether, Babe won five of her eight
events that afternoon.

She tied for first place in another.

Then the team scores were announced.

Babe, the one-woman team, had won the
championship for the Golden Cyclones.

And she had kept the promise she made
to her family.

At age 21, Babe was going to the Olympics.

Los Angeles, 1932

Babe and her Olympic teammates
boarded a train to Los Angeles.
That was where the 1932 Olympic Games
would be held.
The other women played cards
or chatted on the train.

Not Babe.

She didn't want to lose a minute of practice.

She ran in the aisles,

from one end of the train to the other.

Passengers called out,

"Here she comes again!" when they saw her.

In Los Angeles, reporters treated Babe
like a movie star.
But she never forgot why she was there.
She said she had come
to "beat everybody in sight."
To some, it sounded like bragging.
But to those who knew her,
Babe was just being Babe.

Babe would be competing in the javelin,
the high jump, and her old favorite,
the hurdles.
Her new Olympic coach didn't like her
hurdling style.

Most hurdlers put their front leg
out straight when they jumped.
That worked best for narrow hurdles.
But Babe had learned to hurdle
over two-foot-wide hedges.
She still hurdled as if she were
trying to avoid getting scratched.

She kept her front leg up high
and bent at the knee.
The coach told Babe to straighten her leg.
But Babe decided to stick
with what felt right for her.

Babe's first Olympic event

was the javelin throw.

The judges marked the old record

with a small flag on the field.

Babe aimed her javelin right over the flag.

As she threw, her hand slipped.

She felt a pop in her shoulder.

The throw had hurt her.

Would it be good enough?

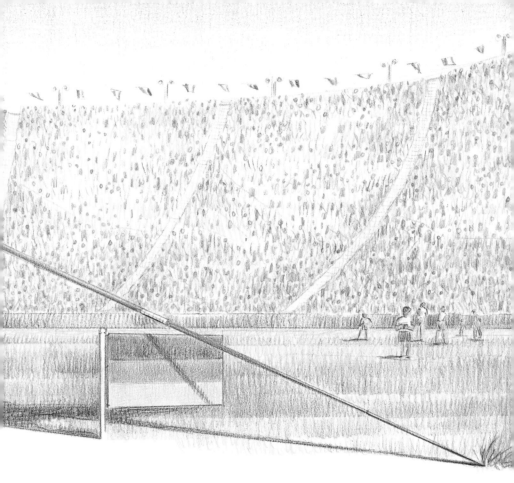

It was, and then some.

The javelin sailed past the flag.

No one else beat her throw.

Babe had set a new world record.

She had also won her first

Olympic gold medal.

Babe had a chance for another medal
in the hurdles a few days later.
The race was a close one.
Babe started late.
She didn't catch up until the fifth hurdle.
Right before the finish,
she pulled ahead of the pack.

She crossed the finish line just inches
ahead of a teammate.
Babe had her second gold medal
and another new world record.
A photo of the race showed Babe
with her front leg bent.
She looked like she was still jumping
those hedges back in Beaumont.

In the high jump, Babe had to settle
for the silver medal.
Both Babe and a teammate
jumped record heights.
Then the judges said that Babe's
highest jump was really a dive.
Her head went over the bar
before her feet did.
That was against the rules.

Babe was never happy
about coming in second.
But her three medals caught the attention
of the whole country.
Babe had made her dream
come true.
She was a star Olympic athlete.

After the Olympics, the city of Dallas
gave a parade in Babe's honor.
Babe and her family rode
in a car covered in roses.
She waved to the cheering crowds.
Even though it was a hot day,
her arms had goosebumps.
Most thrilling of all were the headlines
in newspapers all over the country.
They called Babe the
"World's Greatest Woman Athlete."

Afterword

After Babe finished second in the high jump, the sportswriter Grantland Rice invited her to play golf the next day. She did, and she decided then that she wanted to become a champion golfer.

Babe began training for golf the same way she had trained for track and field. By 1934, she was entering golf tournaments. By 1935, she was winning them. At her peak, Babe won 17 major tournaments in a row. Babe met George Zaharias, a professional wrestler, on a golf course. They were married in 1938.

During her career, Babe Didrikson Zaharias was a pioneer and a role model for women in sports. She helped form the first professional golf association for women. She was named Outstanding Woman Athlete of the Year by the Associated Press six times. In 1950, she was named Outstanding Woman Athlete of the Half Century. Babe really did become one of the greatest athletes that ever lived.

Important Dates

1911—Mildred Ella "Babe" Didrikson is born in Port Arthur, Texas, on June 26.

1917—Didrikson family moves to Beaumont, Texas

1930—Moves to Dallas, Texas, to join the Golden Cyclones

1932—Wins the Amateur Athletic Union track-and-field national championships

1932—Sets three world records and wins two gold medals and one silver medal at the Olympic Games in Los Angeles, California

1934—Enters her first golf tournament

1935—Wins the Texas Women's Amateur Golf Championship

1938—Marries George Zaharias

1946–1947—Wins 17 golf tournaments in a row

1949—Helps found the Ladies Professional Golf Association (LPGA)

1950—Named Outstanding Woman Athlete of the Half Century

1955—Publishes her autobiography, *This Life I've Led*

1956—Died of cancer on September 27 in Galveston, Texas, at the age of 45